Merry Christmas
Rowes

Love,
Brad + John

The BIRD
Alphabet Book

Jerry Pallotta • Illustrated by Edgar Stewart

ini Charlesbridge

To Linda, Jane, and Ellen—J. P.

Text copyright © 1986 by Jerry Pallotta
Illustrations copyright © 1987 by Edgar Stewart
All rights reserved, including the right of reproduction in whole or in part in any form.
Charlesbridge and colophon are registered trademarks of Charlesbridge Publishing, Inc.

Published by Charlesbridge
85 Main Street
Watertown, MA 02472
(617) 926-0329
www.charlesbridge.com

Library of Congress Catalog Card number 89-60423
ISBN-13: 978-0-88106-457-5; ISBN-10: 0-88106-457-2 (hardcover)
ISBN-13: 978-0-88106-451-3; ISBN-10: 0-88106-451-3 (softcover)

Printed in Korea
(hc) 10 9 8 7 6 5 4 3 2
(sc) 10 9 8 7 6 5 4 3 2

Special thanks to Brian Cassie.

A is for Atlantic Puffin.
Atlantic Puffins have colorful beaks.
They live on the ocean almost all year. When nesting
on land, they are found in groups called colonies.

A a

B is for Bat. Hey, wait a second! Bats are not birds. Bats are mammals. Even though they have wings and they can fly, they do not have feathers. Get out of this book, you Bats!

B b

Now that the Bats are gone, let's find a
bird whose name begins with the letter B.

B b

B is for Blue-footed Booby. Boobies are sea birds. They can be found eating fish, which they catch by diving into the ocean. The other bird on this page is a Red-footed Booby.

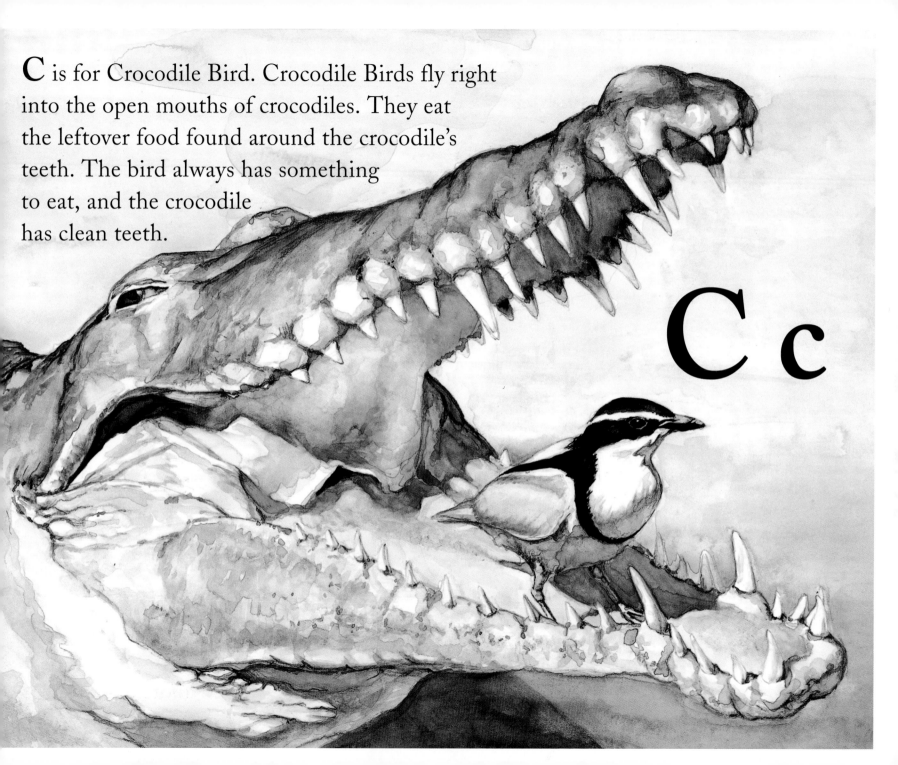

C is for Crocodile Bird. Crocodile Birds fly right into the open mouths of crocodiles. They eat the leftover food found around the crocodile's teeth. The bird always has something to eat, and the crocodile has clean teeth.

C c

D is for Duck. There are many different kinds of ducks. There are Wood Ducks, Mallards, Pintails, Black Ducks, Harlequin Ducks, Canvasbacks, Ruddy Ducks, Masked Ducks, Ring-necked Ducks and many more.

D d

E e

E is for Eagle. These Eagles are Bald Eagles, but they are not really bald. Their heads are covered with beautiful white feathers. The Bald Eagle is the National Emblem of the United States, and it can be seen on the back of a quarter and a dollar bill.

F is for Flamingo. Flamingos have very long necks and very long legs. Their beaks are curved, and sometimes they like to stand on one leg.

G g

G is for Gosling. Goslings are baby geese. When they are young, they like to follow their parents around. The birds on this page are called Canada Geese.

H h

H is for Hummingbird. Hummingbirds
are tiny birds that fly really fast. Their long
beaks are perfect for sucking nectar out of flowers.

I i

I is for Indigo Bunting.
The male Indigo Bunting is
beautifully bright blue from its
head to the tip of its tail. The female
is plain-colored, so that it is hard to
find when it sits in its nest.

J j

J is for Jacana. Wow! What big feet! Jacanas have feet that are just right for standing on lily pads. They are also called Lily-trotters.

K k

K is for Kiwi. The Kiwi is a bird that cannot fly. It has wings. It lays eggs. It has a beak and it has feathers just like other birds. But if it wants to go somewhere, it has to walk.

L l

L is for Lovebird. These birds are very colorful. They are called Lovebirds because they like to sit close together. They usually look like they are hugging and kissing each other.

M is for Meadowlark. Meadowlarks build their hard-to-find nests on the ground. People love Meadowlarks because they sing cheerfully for hours at a time.

M
m

N n

N is for Northern Cardinal. This is one of the few birds that is almost entirely red. Sometimes it is simply called a "Redbird."

O is for Oystercatcher. This bird is able to stick its beak into oysters and clams and pry them open. It lives near coastal mudflats where it can find plenty of shellfish to eat.

O o

P is for Penguin. Penguins cannot fly in the sky. It is fun to watch them swim, because it looks like they are flying when they are underwater.

P p

Q q

Q is for Quetzal. The Quetzal is a bright green bird with an extremely long tail. It is found in Central America. Because there are so few of these birds, they are considered to be an endangered species.

R r

R is for Roadrunner. Roadrunners can fly when they want to, but they usually prefer to run. Roadrunners live in the desert, and they chase and catch little lizards for food.

S s

S is for Spoonbill. Can you believe it? This bird has a bill that looks just like a spoon. The baby Spoonbills do not grow their wide spoon-shaped bills until they get older.

T is for Toucan. The Toucan has a very long and wide beak. Its beak is so big that you might think a Toucan would not be able to fly. However, the beak is really not very heavy.

U is for Umbrellabird. This is a black jungle bird. The feathers around the top of its head are shaped like an umbrella, but when it rains the umbrella does not keep its head dry.

U
u

V is for Vulture.
Vultures have hardly
any feathers on their
heads. Maybe vultures
are the birds that
should be called bald.

V v

W is for White-faced Scops Owl. This owl lives in Africa. It hides in trees waiting for a chance to swoop down on insects and other small creatures. Owls make very little noise when they fly.

W w

X is for Xenops. This is probably the only bird whose name begins with X. Unlike most birds, the Xenops has a beak that is curved upwards.

X x

Y y

Y is for Yellow-bellied Sapsucker. The Yellow-bellied Sapsucker is a woodpecker that got its crazy name because it drinks sap out of its favorite trees. It has a tongue with a brushlike tip.

Z z

Z is for Zillions of Zebra Finches. These Australian birds have pretty black and white striped tails.

The End